This not

belongs to:

....

Made in the USA
Las Vegas, NV
29 July 2021

27211819R00073